Travel Through the British Isles

Lynn Huggins-Cooper

QED Publishing

Written by: Lynn Huggins-Cooper
Designed by: Manishi Varshney (Q2A Media)
Editor: Honor Head
Picture Researcher: Sujatha Menon (Q2A Media)

Publisher Steve Evans
Creative Director Zeta Davies
Senior Editor Hannah Ray

Printed and bound in China

Picture credits

Key: t = top, b = bottom, m = middle,
l = left, r = right, FC = front cover

Science Photo Library/ Photolibrary: 4 (background), 9t, 18b, Carsten Reisinger/ Shutterstock:
4t, 4br, Dimitrios Kaisaris/ Shutterstock: 4m, Dkessaris | Dreamstime.com: 4bl, Matthew Dixon/
Istockphoto: 6b, Gareth McCormack/ Lonely Planet Images: 7tl, 7tr, Eoin Clarke/ Lonely Planet
Images: 7b, Bethune Carmichae/ Lonely Planet Images: 8, Nina Pope: 9b, Manfred Gottschalk/
Lonely Planet Images: 10b, Pearl Bucknall/ PhotolibraryWales.com: 11t, Neil Setchfield / Lonely
Planet Images: 11b, PAUL GLENDELL / Still Pictures: 12t, Robert Harding Picture Library
Ltd/ Photolibrary: 12b, Nicholas Reuss/ Lonely Planet Images: 13m, Rachael: 14t, Thomas Bendy/
Istockphoto: 14b, Index Stock Imagery/ Photolibrary: 15t, Nathan Middleton/ Fotolibra: 16t,
Patrick Ward/CORBIS: 16b, Jtb Photo Communications Inc/ Photolibrary: 17t, Tim Page/CORBIS:
19t, Huw Jones, HLJ Photography: 19b, Glenn Miles/ Fotolibra: 20b, Jon Davison/ Lonely Planet
Images: 21t, Dale O'Dell / Alamy: 21b, David Robertson Photography, photographersdirect.
com: 23t, Kit Houghton/CORBIS: 23b, Patrick Horton/ Lonely Planet Images: 24b, Graeme
Cornwallis/ Lonely Planet Images: 25t, Christer Fredriksson/ Lonely Planet Images: 25b, Oxford
Scientific Films/ Photolibrary: 26b, Linda Wright/ Fotolibra: 27t, Paul Glendell / Alamy: 27b.

Words in **bold** can be found in the glossary on page 31.

Contents

Atlantic
Ocean

Shetland Islands

Orkney Islands

Wick

SCOTLAND

Outer Hebrides

Skye

Aberdeen

Inner
Hebrides

NORTHERN IRELAND

Edinburgh

Farne Islands

Isles of Arran

North Sea

Derry

Newcastle

Sligo

Belfast

Isle of Man

York

Hull

Irish Sea

Galway

Dublin

Anglesey

Liverpool

ENGLAND

Aran Islands

Llandudno

Limerick

Birmingham

Kerry

Cambridge

Cork

Oxford

REPUBLIC
OF IRELAND

Cardiff

London

WALES

Bath

Dover

Brighton

Lands End

Isle of Wight

Plymouth

English Channel

Isles of Scilly

Where in the world are the British Isles?

The British Isles is a group of islands in north-west Europe. It includes the large islands of Great Britain (made up of Wales, England and Scotland) and Ireland (made up of Northern Ireland and the Republic of Ireland – also known as Eire). There are also many smaller surrounding islands, such as the Isle of Man, the Inner and Outer Hebrides, the Isles of Scilly, the Channel Islands, the Isle of Wight, the Farne Islands, the Aran Islands, Anglesey and the Orkneys.

Though it does not cover a particularly large area, as you travel through the British Isles you will experience an exciting mix of different landscapes, climates, peoples, foods and traditions.

What are the British Isles like?

Travelling through the British Isles you will see a mixture of old and new. The British Isles has a long history so there are many ancient monuments and historic buildings to visit. Scattered throughout the countryside, you will see traditional, old villages with **thatched** cottages and **beamed** buildings. But there are also many large, lively cities to visit, too, with plenty of exciting things to see and do.

Caernarfon Castle in Wales is one of the many castles to visit in the British Isles.

Tourists love to visit Tower bridge, built over the River Thames in London, in 1894.

6

The British Isles has many beautiful bays and beaches. This lovely, sandy beach is at Keem Strand in County Mayo, in the Republic of Ireland.

Landscapes

There are many different types of landscapes in the British Isles. You can trek across **moorland** in Devon, in south-west England, or go hill walking in the Lake District in northern England. You can visit a variety of coastal habitats, from craggy cliffs and rockpools to beautiful beaches in the west of Ireland. There is also wonderful woodland to enjoy – such as the Caledonian Forest in Scotland.

Multicultural Britain

Since the 1950s, the British Isles has become a **multicultural** society. Many people have **emigrated** to the British Isles to live and work. As you travel through the towns and cities of the British Isles, you will see the ways that people from all over the world have enriched the British Isles with their culture and customs.

Over 6000 islands make up the British Isles

Hiking is popular and there are many hills to explore, such as the Aonach Eagach near Glencoe, in Scotland.

Climate

The British Isles has many different climates, from the **sub-tropical** warmth of the Isles of Scilly in the path of the **Gulf Stream**, to the colder temperatures of the beautiful Orkney Islands off the coast of Scotland.

Food and drink

Many people in the British Isles buy and cook food from big supermarkets. Here you will see food that has been flown in from all around the world, but there are still many small shops and restaurants which sell local specialities.

As well as a full English breakfast you can also get a full Scottish, a full Welsh and a full Irish breakfast, which all include slightly different foods.

Regional dishes

In Wales, you might see laver bread or 'bara lawr' on menus. This bread is made from seaweed collected at low tide and boiled to make a type of jelly. The jelly is mixed with oats and lots of seasoning and is then made into **patties** and fried. If you ask for bread rolls in a bakery in Newcastle, you may get stottie cakes. These aren't actually cakes but thick, large, flat bread rolls. If you went to Scotland, you might try haggis. This is meat, spices and oatmeal stuffed into a case, like a sausage. It is usually served with neeps and tatties – mashed swede and potatoes.

Haggis is a savoury pudding traditionally made from sheep's 'pluck' – the heart, liver and lungs. Today, vegetarian haggis is also available.

Big breakfast

If you order a full English breakfast in a café, you would receive a plate loaded with some or all of the following: bacon, eggs, sausages, fried bread, fried tomatoes, mushrooms, **bubble and squeak**, **black pudding** and baked beans.

Fish and chips

At the seaside, you might fancy some fish and chips. This is fish fried in batter and served with thick potato chips. Fish and chips can be bought in most towns in the British Isles – but many people think they taste best eaten on a windy beach!

Last week I went to visit Grandad in Devon. We went for a long walk along the beach and explored the rockpools. Grandad said that the fresh air had given him an appetite, so we went to a tea shop and had a Devon cream tea. I had two scones, which are like small, plain cakes. They are served with a little dish of strawberry jam and a little dish of **clotted cream**. You cut the scones in half and fill them with jam and cream – yum!

Ben

Fish and chips have been popular all over the British Isles since Victorian times. Salt and vinegar is usually added.

Getting about

As in many European countries, lots of people in the British Isles travel by car. There are many big motorways that make travelling from place to place easy, but traffic can be heavy, especially around large cities. You can also travel around the British Isles using trains, coaches and buses. Many cities also have underground railways, such as the London Underground and the Tyneside Metro system.

Planes and boats

There are lots of small **regional** airports as well as larger, well-known ones, such as Heathrow in London. You can take both internal flights from one area of the British Isles to another, or fly abroad. A ferry can take you to Ireland and to many of the smaller islands of the British Isles, such as the Isle of Wight. **Hovercrafts** and **hydrofoils** also hop backwards and forwards between the British Isles and mainland Europe.

The Snowdon Mountain Railway was built in 1896.

You can travel from the British Isles to mainland Europe on a ferry.

P&O Stena

Take the train

You can travel all over the British Isles by train, which is a great way to see the scenery. There are even a few old steam trains that run for tourists, such as the Snowdon Mountain Railway in Wales. The Channel Tunnel, built under the English Channel, links the British Isles with France and Belgium.

I've just got back from my school trip to London. We went to loads of museums. The London Underground train system is amazing. It's incredible to think you can travel all over London through tunnels beneath the ground! We took a trip down the Thames on a riverboat. A guide told us about all the things you could see. My favourite was the view of the Tower of London, the old palace and prison owned for centuries by the kings and queens of England. The guide told us lots of spooky stories about headless queens, prisoners and ghosts!
Love
Eleanor

Some of the riverboats on the River Thames, in London, have restaurants. People enjoy a meal as they cruise along.

The coast

As you travel around the coastline of the British Isles, you will see many different types of landscapes and animals, as well as many seaside towns and cities.

Coastal creatures

The coastline of Scotland is very rugged and is made up of beautiful beaches and spectacular, rocky cliffs. Many different types of animals live around the Scottish coast. You can see countless seabirds, both common and grey seals, and other sea creatures, such as whales, porpoises, dolphins and basking sharks.

Many seaside towns and cities have piers. Brighton pier, in the south-east of England, was built in Victorian times and is still in use today.

PALACE PIER

FREE

TO TAKE AWAY
FISH & CHIPS   TEA
SAUSAGES   COFFEE
CHOCOLATE

Puffins are found in parts of the British Isles, such as the Farne Islands off the coast of Northumbria.

Wonderful Wales

If you visit the Gower Peninsula in Wales, you will find many beautiful beaches and coves. There are limestone cliffs to walk along and stretches of sandy beach to play on. In some places, such as Llangennith Sands, you can even go surfing.

The *tiny* Channel Island of Herm has a beach made of shells that were carried there by the Gulf Stream

Brighton is brilliant! I went with my family last weekend. We went on the pier and I won a cuddly dolphin on the tin-can alley game. Afterwards, we had hot doughnuts, fresh from the pan. They were great, but I got covered in sugar. I went on a ride which swung out over the sea and was really scary! Then mum said she wanted to go for a walk through The Lanes, some tiny, twisty streets with amazing shops. After lunch in a smart café, we went to the Royal Pavilion, which was very cool! It is an Indian-style palace that George, Prince Regent (who became King George IV of England in 1820) had remodelled so he had somewhere to stay when he came to visit.
Love Beth

At Rhossili Bay, on the Gower Peninsula in Wales, huge waves roar in from the Atlantic Ocean, making the beaches great for surfers!

Capital cities

Gorgeous murals and gold leaf decorate many walls inside the magnificent Cardiff Castle.

As you travel through the cities of the British Isles, you will see that each capital has its own style, from bustling London to elegant Dublin.

London

In London, it is easy for visitors to imagine they are on a film set, especially when they visit Buckingham Palace where the Queen lives, or parliament at Whitehall. However, London is not just for tourists. Seven and a half million people live and work in this busy capital city.

The Swiss Re Tower in the financial district of London is known as 'The Gherkin' because of its unusual shape.

Cardiff

The capital city of Wales is Cardiff (*Caerdydd* in Welsh). There is lots to see and do. You can visit Cardiff Castle, which has the remains of a Roman settlement and a Norman castle. *Techniquest*, in the Cardiff Bay area, has a Science Discovery Centre with 160 interactive exhibits and a Planetarium.

Dublin

Dublin, or *Baile Átha Cliath* in Gaelic, is the capital of the Republic of Ireland. It has many historic buildings and wide, tree-lined streets. Dublin Castle stands on the site of a Viking fortress. A castle of some type has stood there ever since.

Edinburgh

There are many historic buildings, such as Edinburgh Castle and the shops on the Royal Mile in the capital city of Scotland (*Dùn Èideann* in Gaelic). It is well known for the Edinburgh Festival, held in August, when thousands of visitors flock to see a wide variety of dancers, musicians and actors performing.

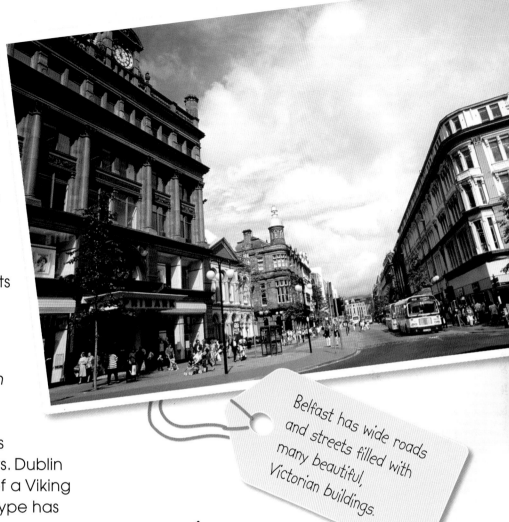

Belfast has wide roads and streets filled with many beautiful, Victorian buildings.

Belfast

The capital of Northern Ireland is on the mouth of the River Lagan. The world's largest **dry dock** is in Belfast, and it is where the ship *Titanic* was built. The centre of Belfast is for pedestrians only, so it is relaxing to wander around without worrying about traffic. There are lots of shops to explore, and Victorian architecture and sculptures to look at.

 YOU'VE GOT MAIL

Hi! We visited Cardiff Castle today – it looks like a medieval fairytale castle! We had a tour of the apartments and clock tower, and then went to a banquet in the undercroft – it's the place where the bodies of important people would be kept and buried after they died. There were people dressed up in medieval costumes singing as we ate. Tina x

Heritage and history

The British Isles has a long history, full of invaders and settlers. There are many castles and **fortifications** in the British Isles that tell the story of wars and battles fought against these invaders.

Picts

Hadrian's Wall in Northumbria is an 118km long wall built in Roman times to keep a fierce tribe called the **Picts** from invading the rest of England. It stretched from the west to the east coast.

Celts

Ireland has many sites where you can see remains left behind by the tribes who lived there from 2500 BCE. There are many stone circles and tombs. Some stone circles are places where ancient **Celts** used to worship their gods.

Hadrian, a Roman Emperor in 117 CE, invaded Britain and gave orders to build the famous wall.

Walk with Shakespeare

If you go to Stratford-upon-Avon, in central England, you can visit many historic buildings, including the birthplace of the playwright William Shakespeare. This is a lovely, old beamed building – and it is incredible to think that you can walk in rooms where Shakespeare walked nearly 450 years ago. Shakespeare's plays are still performed in Stratford-upon-Avon's three theatres, and also in the Globe Theatre, by the River Thames in London. The Globe Theatre was rebuilt on the original site where many of Shakespeare's plays were first acted.

See, hear and smell

Further north, you can visit the city of York with its Viking remains. The Jorvik Viking Centre tells the story of the Viking invasion and settlement in the British Isles. There is a 'sight and sound' display to ride around – with rather stinky smells of the time, too!

Hadrian's Wall is one of my favourite places to visit. You can see it stretching away, far into the distance. You can try on some armour at a Roman museum called Vindolanda. There is a re-creation of a Roman banquet and guess what, they ate stuffed dormice!

Love, Iona

17

Farming in the British Isles

Orchards are found all over the British Isles. Apples are grown for eating, cooking and making into cider, an alcoholic drink.

As you travel around the British Isles, you will see lots of open farmland. About three-quarters of the land in the British Isles is used for a mixture of **arable** and **livestock** farming.

Many working farms in the British Isles ha[ve] holiday cottages where you can stay and even help out on the farm.

Sheep in the hills

Sheep are farmed all over the British Isles, even in wild, mountainous areas such as the hill farms in Wales. Many farmers round up their sheep using trained Border Collie dogs.

Sheep are farmed for wool, sheepskin fleeces, meat and milk.

Fruits and vegetables

Many different crops are grown in the British Isles, such as wheat, corn and barley, as well as vegetables. There are also orchards full of apples and pears. Lots of soft fruit, such as strawberries and raspberries, are grown and many farms have 'pick your own' schemes, which means you pay a fee and then collect your own fruit, fresh from the fields.

Organic food

You can now buy lots of organically grown food – that means that no chemicals have been used on the crops. Lots of this food is sold at farmers' markets around the British Isles. Farmers and **smallholders** bring their goods to sell directly to the public at the markets.

I've been helping Mum with the harvest on our farm. I seem to have picked hundreds and hundreds of apples! We are taking all the apples to a farmers' market in Durham, in northern England. People come from all over to buy our apples because they're organic, and they're old English varieties such as 'Ribstone Pippin' and 'Knobby Russet' that you can't buy in the supermarkets any more.

Mum and I are taking the horsebox down to the National Fruit Collection at Brogdale, in Kent, next week – this is a special collection of fruit trees and bushes and it's the largest collection of varieties of fruit trees in the world. We plan to buy some new trees to make the orchard even bigger. We'll need the horsebox to bring them home.
Alex

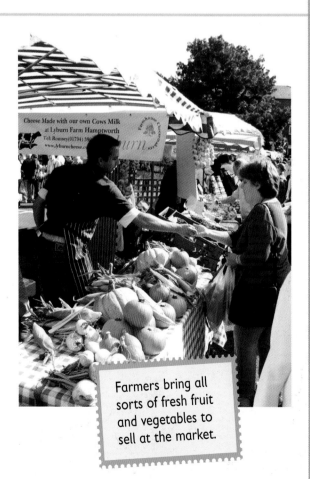

Farmers bring all sorts of fresh fruit and vegetables to sell at the market.

Myths and legends of the British Isles

The British Isles has a fine storytelling tradition, full of tales of brave heroes and fierce monsters.

Busy giant

In Ireland, you'll hear tales of Celtic heroes such as the giant, Fionn Mac Cumhaill. The myth says that the Giant's Causeway in County Antrim, Northern Ireland, was made when Fionn decided to build a bridge across the sea between Ireland and Scotland. Another legend says he threw a clod of earth at a Scottish giant. The earth landed in the sea and became the Isle of Man.

Giant killer

Natural features all over the British Isles have inspired storytellers. St Michael's Mount in Cornwall, south-west England, is a tiny island that can be reached by a causeway only at low tide. Set on a rocky, granite crag, it is said to be the place where a fearsome giant called Cormoran lived and terrorized the local people. Legend tells of a farmer's son named Jack, who is said to have lured Cormoran away from the Mount and trapped him in a huge pit. Jack the Giant Killer then travelled round the British Isles, killing other giants.

The Giant's Causeway is a stone structure made from volcanic rock.

King Arthur

If you travel to Somerset, you will hear about Glastonbury Tor (tor means 'rocky hill'). It is said to be the sacred Isle of Avalon, where King Arthur was taken after he fought with the evil sorcerer, Mordred. King Arthur was the legendary king who gathered at the famous Round Table with his knights. The legend says Arthur still waits on Avalon for the day when Britain needs a hero.

The Tower of St Michael at Glastonbury Tor.

Loch Ness is an amazing 38km long and on average 2km wide. It is up to 225m deep.

Loch Ness monster

No visit to Scotland would be complete without a visit to **Loch** Ness to look for the monster which is said to live there. Some people even think the monster is a dinosaur, left over from prehistoric times. Many people claim to have seen the monster but no one has ever been able to prove that the monster really exists.

Some people think Nessie may be a stray seal – or even a dinosaur!

Festivals and holidays

The British Isles has many different festivals and fairs. As you travel from place to place, you can see traditions that have survived to the present day.

Bonfire Night

On 5 November the British Isles is lit up with bonfires and fireworks. Bonfire Night remembers the discovery of a plan to blow up parliament by a man called Guy Fawkes in 1605. The plan was called The Gunpowder Plot. As you travel from town to town, you may see a 'Guy' on many bonfires. The Guy is like a scarecrow and is burned on the fire.

In Lewes, in East Sussex in England, a great parade is held on Bonfire Night. Many people dress up in historical costume.

Lewes has many Bonfire Societies who all take part in the celebrations on 5 November

Hogmanay

In Scotland, Christmas is celebrated in much the same way as the rest of the British Isles. But it is at Hogmanay, which brings in the New Year on the night of 31 December, when the biggest celebrations take place, with street parties and lively processions.

Fireballs

Throughout the British Isles, amazing Fire Ceremonies take place that are linked with the **Winter Solstice**, or midwinter. At Stonehaven, on the north-east coast of Scotland, you can see giant fireballs being swung around on long metal poles.

Spectacular firework displays light up the sky on Hogmanay.

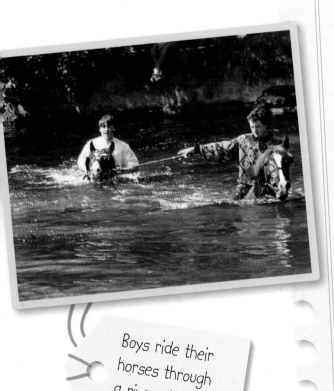

Boys ride their horses through a river at the Appleby Fair.

This weekend I went to Appleby Fair in Cumbria (in the north of England) with Grandad. He's been coming since he was a little boy. We went all the way in Grandad's vardo - an old-fashioned gypsy caravan. My horse Khola pulled the wagon all the way to Appleby. Grandad said there's been a gypsy horse fair at Appleby since 1685. There were lots of travellers selling horses and having trotting races. There were boys 'flashing' the ponies – galloping them down the lanes near the fair, so people could see them. It was a bit scary! Down in the town, people were riding the horses across the river.
Ellie x

Climate

The British Isles has a temperate climate. That means it does not have extreme weather conditions. However, a temperate climate is often very changeable, so even in summer it can be sunny one day and rainy the next. Sensible visitors to the British Isles always carry an umbrella!

Seasons

The British Isles has very clear seasons. If you travel there in spring, it will be cool with showers and a little sunshine. Bulbs such as daffodils and tulips come into flower at this time. Summer can be hot, especially in areas such as the Isles of Scilly. Autumn in the British Isles is lovely, as the leaves change to gold and red. Winter can be very cold indeed.

People walk in the woods in the autumn to see the changing leaves.

In the far north of the British Isles, snowfall can be deep during the winter.

Snowy weather

There are some differences in climate as you travel through the British Isles. The north of Scotland, for example, tends to get colder, longer winters than the south of England. Heavy, lasting snowfall is only likely in the northern parts of the British Isles, or on high ground such as in Snowdonia, in Wales.

Warm air

In general, the British climate is mild for its **latitude**. This is because of the Gulf Stream, a warm ocean current that starts out in the Gulf of Mexico and flows across the Atlantic ocean.

The temperature in the British Isles can be as high as 30°C in summer and below freezing in winter.

Summer holidays at the seaside in the British Isles are still popular.

Conservation and the environment

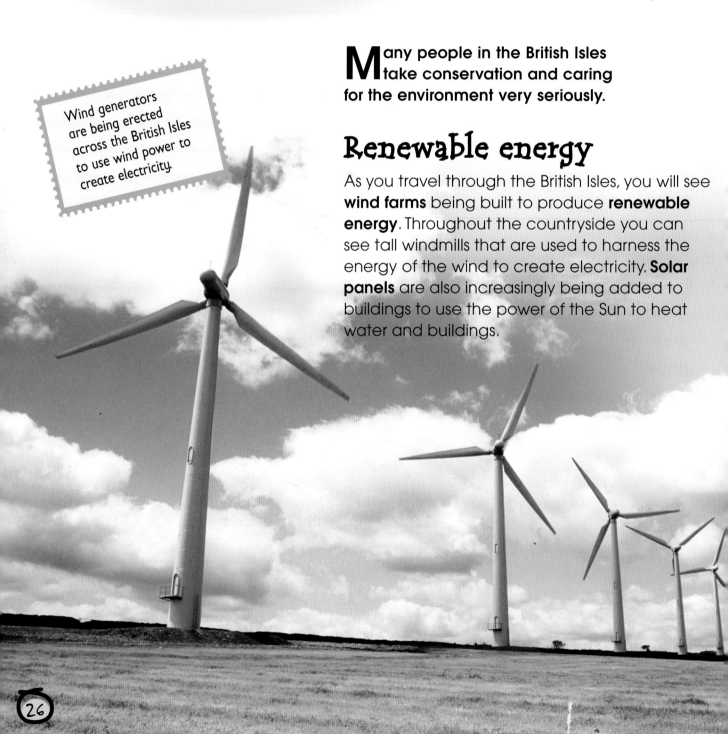

Wind generators are being erected across the British Isles to use wind power to create electricity.

Many people in the British Isles take conservation and caring for the environment very seriously.

Renewable energy

As you travel through the British Isles, you will see **wind farms** being built to produce **renewable energy**. Throughout the countryside you can see tall windmills that are used to harness the energy of the wind to create electricity. **Solar panels** are also increasingly being added to buildings to use the power of the Sun to heat water and buildings.

Recycling

The government is taking steps to greatly reduce the amount of waste sent to **landfill sites**, where it rots slowly and releases poisonous chemicals and **greenhouse gases** into the air. Many local councils collect plastics, paper, glass and tins to recycle, and give householders free compost bins to collect kitchen waste to use in the garden.

Freecycle

All over the British Isles there are local **freecycle** groups. These groups encourage people to give away possessions they don't want to people who need them. If you have an item you no longer want, you add it to an email list. If somebody wants your item, they reply and come and collect it. This saves the possessions from being taken to landfill sites, and helps the environment as well as other people.

I have joined the Conservation Club at school. This week we have been finding out about The Wildlife Trusts. Many plant and animal species in the British Isles, such as the Red Kite, are protected by law so that they do not become extinct. The Wildlife Trusts tells people how to help look after these animals and even how to to build special habitats or places for creatures and plants to live, either in nature reserves or in their own gardens.
Ruby

At the weekend, my cub scout troop took part in a 'clean beaches' campaign to collect litter left on the coast. Sadly, we found a lot. We are making posters for our website to show the dangers of pollution to sea life, as well as the effect litter has on tourism and the livelihoods of fishermen.
Mike

Activity ideas

1   Make a 3D map of the British Isles using papier mâché. Draw the rough shape on a sheet of card, and add pieces of crumpled paper, glued firmly in place. Coat the model in PVA glue, and cover the whole model carefully with tissue paper. Push the paper carefully into all the inlets and coves you have created. Repeat this step until you have a smooth surface and leave to dry. Then paint and label your model.

2   Find a recipe for regional food from the British Isles – the Internet is a good source. With an adult, cook the food and eat a typical British meal. You could also buy some examples of regional foods and sample them, before reviewing them and displaying the reports of the 'food critics'.

NOTE FOR ADULTS: Please ensure that children do not suffer from any food allergies before making or eating any food.

3   Make a fact file about the Channel Tunnel – and then make a model. Make the tunnel by bending a sheet of thin card into a tunnel shape and attaching it to a base – the side from a strong cardboard box will do, or a large piece of corrugated cardboard. Paint the model with brown paint mixed with a little PVA glue for strength. Tear strips of blue tissue, crêpe and cellophane in shades of blue and stick them to the base board, on either side of the tunnel – this will be the sea. You could even add clay sea creatures!

4   Using travel brochures, cut out pictures and make a collage to show the image of the British Isles given to tourists. What ideas and images do travel agents use to 'sell' the British Isles as a travel destination? Make a list of 10 words used in the brochures to persuade people to visit the British Isles.

5 Carry out research using the Internet, magazines and newspapers to find out more about renewable energy in the British Isles. Use your information to debate with friends or classmates 'for' and 'against' renewable energy.

6 With an adult, visit a local farmers' market and see how far the food has travelled before you buy it. Compare these 'food miles' with food bought at the supermarket.

7 Plan a trip round the British Isles! If you could pick ten places, where would you go? Why? How would you travel around?

8 Using a word-processing computer program, make a booklet showing the different types of coastal features you find around Britain. These should include cliffs, rocky beaches and sand dunes – you will be amazed at how many you can find. Cut and paste photos from the Internet and place them with the text. Print your fact file.

9 Interview people, such as parents and grandparents, about holidays they have taken in the British Isles. Why did they choose to take their holiday in the British Isles? Record the answers on tape or video and edit your recording to make a documentary.

10 Using books, the Internet and travel brochures, research one of the smaller islands of the British Isles, such as Herm. How big is the island? How many people live there? What is the landscape like? Does it have any special festivals and traditions?

11 Do an Internet search to find out about different island groups around the world. Do they have as many islands as the British Isles?

12 Find other places on the same latitude as the British Isles. Find out if the average temperatures are the same, or if they differ. Plot the results on a chart to compare the temperatures in the different places.

13 Using books and websites, find out about the beaches of the British Isles, and make a fact file. Make sections on tourism, wildlife, geology – or anything you find interesting.

14 Find out about where people came from when they emigrated to the British Isles in the 20th century. Why did people come to the British Isles? Make a world map and mark the countries people came from.

15 Imagine you are travelling across the British Isles. Write entries in an imaginary blog about your journey. What do you see? Who do you meet? Does anything funny happen to you? What do you learn about the British Isles?

16 Write a tourist leaflet describing a city in the British Isles. Remember to use exciting language to encourage people to visit.

17 Find out more about Hadrian's Wall from the English Heritage website. Then make a clay model of the wall.

18 Read some of Shakespeare's plays. You don't have to read the original versions – *Mr William Shakespeare's Plays* by Marcia Williams is a great introduction; *Shakespeare Stories*, written by Leon Garfield and illustrated by Michael Foreman, tells the stories in an easy-to-understand way.

19 Do a web search about landfill sites and their dangers. Make a poster about alternatives to landfill sites, including ways to reduce waste, such as recycling and reusing objects.

20 Find out more about Scottish Hogmanay traditions. Write a report as though you spent Hogmanay in Scotland and experienced it for yourself.

Glossary

arable Land used for growing crops.

beamed Made from large pieces of timber. You can often see wooden beams both outside and inside very old houses.

black pudding A type of sausage made from pork fat and pigs' blood.

bubble and squeak Leftover vegetables that are mixed together and fried.

Celts Ancient peoples who lived in parts of the British Isles.

clotted cream Very thick cream.

dry dock A dock that can be drained of water and kept dry while work is being done on a boat.

emigrated Having left one area or country to live in another.

fortifications Thick walls or other ways to make a place safe from attack.

freecycle An organization that helps people to pass on things to other people rather than throw them away.

greenhouse gases Any of the gases in the atmosphere that contribute to global warming.

Gulf Stream A warm ocean current that flows north from the Gulf of Mexico through to the Atlantic Ocean.

hovercraft A boat driven by a propeller that has a cushion of air underneath. The cushion of air allows it to skim across the water.

hydrofoil A boat that travels across the water very fast by skimming across the surface.

landfill sites Where rubbish is dumped and then buried.

latitude Distance from the equator (an imaginary circle around the middle of the Earth, shown on most maps).

livestock Animals kept on a farm.

loch Scottish word for a very deep lake.

moorland An area of open land usually covered in coarse grass, bracken, heather and moss.

multicultural Made up of people from many different cultural backgrounds.

patties Small, flat cakes.

Picts Ancient people of northern Britain.

regional From a particular area or place.

renewable energy 'Green' energy, such as solar or wind power, that will never run out.

smallholder A person who has a small farm and keeps animals and/or grows vegetables.

solar panels Panels that trap and use the heat from sunlight.

sub-tropical When the climate is hot in the summer and the winters are mild and rainy.

temperate When the weather is never very hot nor very cold.

thatched When the roof of a cottage or house is made of straw.

wind farms Collections of wind turbines that generate electricity using the power of the wind.

Winter Solstice A winter festival that happens on or about 22 December in the Northern Hemisphere.

Index